Dedication

I dedicate this book to Almighty God for giving me the insights and knowledge to be able to carry out this work completely.

About Author: Great Omordia born on the 5th of April 1997 in the south eastern part of Nigeria, an aspiring writer with a creative and innovative mind, WHO ARE YOU?   is his debut book.

WHO ARE YOU? ??

Chapter 1 - Who are you? The question

When faced with this question, how do we answer?

Most people go about saying what they have and what they've achieved, but is that really who we are? I believe one cannot truly define themselves if they associate it with material things or achievements, the truth is with hard work and dedication anybody can get those things.

What makes you you, is what nobody has or can get no matter how hard they try or work or how many figures their bank account carries, just like finger prints we are all unique in our own way, we do not grow into who we are neither does our past experience make us who we are, just as we were born with our minds, we were also born with who we are. Not everybody asks themselves who they are in fact majority of people come across that question when asked by someone else but usually in different aspect.

Sometimes you say to someone "ask yourself that" so who is yourself if you asking the question isn't?

The reality of who we are isn't always visible to us, it takes a lot of self awareness to be able to find who we really are, some people believe the purpose of their existence is who they are, i am telling you it is a different thing to know who you are and what your purpose in life is, confusing it will make it harder to know who we really are because they are somewhat interwoven and can easily be mistaken for the same thing, finding out who we are can help us find our true purpose in life but no way is it the same thing. there are shortcuts to finding our purpose in life, finding our purpose in life can be quickened by knowing what we have passion in, our potentials, skills and dreams but all that never tells us who we are, finding our purpose in life will make us happy and joyous but finding out who you are doesn't always come out as we expect, the truth behind who we really are can either be terrifying or enticing depending on the type of person we've grown into.

Finding out who we are can be tough because sometimes we have to contradict ourselves to be able to make a clearer connection to who we are and most times we don't always pay attention to who we are just who we want to become which is a good thing actually but it leaves the question unanswered, to be able to better ourselves it is best we know who we really are underneath our names,titles and achievements. You see nobody can tell who you really are no matter how close they are to you how long you've been together because your personality isn't who you are, what you've made yourself become and the people you interact with, our experiences in life are things that shape our personality, only you can know who you really are, you can tell it to other people you can try to show them but the truth is they can never know completely because we ourselves can't fully know who we are that is why sometimes we surprise ourselves, Times like that is when the real you underneath the you, you've made yourself to become shoves you aside to make a decision or act on something because you are just going to blow it off and it doesn't want that. Our minds help us think and make decisions, make plans, creates, destroy, positive thinking and negative thinking all in our minds, it is a powerful tool that we are gifted with, our mind can play tricks on us, it can make us see things differently, it can blind us, it can help us, our mind is more powerful than we are because we follow it blindly sometimes it makes us do what we will regret even when knowing we will, we still tend to do it because the mind is already up, we think negative things knowing well enough that positive thinking is what we need but the mind comes out with the negativity and you can't help it but that's only because we don't let who we are take control, when you find who you really are your mind becomes your servant and obeys everything you want and stops acting on his own.

We are made up of three main parts : the mind, the body and our inner self.

These three parts are a part of us that makes decisions on their own, the will to do whatsoever they please. I'm going to talk about all three parts separately to better our understanding on what makes us whole as a human being.

1: The mind : The mind is an extension of us a brilliant part of us and a powerful part of who we are because it has the power to destroy us and also build us, a wicked master and a loyal servant, the most creative part of who we are.

2: The body : The body is a dumb part of us that does what makes us feel good at the moment and not care about what happens next, the body can easily be manipulated by every nice things that we come across because that is what the body is mainly concerned about. Its the dumbest part of who we are and because of that it is protected and supported by the other parts when necessary.

3: Our inner self : This is who we really are, the part of us that is uncontrollable but mostly suppressed doesn't like to interfere unless consulted or extremely necessary, the part of us that is always right in everything, some call it intuition, gut feelings, hunch or instinct but its our inner self who we really are trying to reach out because its suppressed and sometimes what it's trying to say to us isn't usually clear because of its suppression and our lack of attentiveness.

The body and the mind are best friends, they work together hand in hand well most of the time, the mind doesn't rely on the body as much as the body relies on the mind, the body also makes decisions on its own even when the mind is against it, for example someone trying to loose some weight knowing well eating too much won't promote the goal but the body wants the food anyway another example is someone who is very in love with a particular person but can't stop sleeping around with other people not because of love for the other people but because the body wants it and at the end of the day he/she regrets it. We can make our mind and body work together and always make decisions that is best for us but sometimes the mind just acts on its own and brings thoughts we don't want, the best way to insure that our mind and body doesn't do what we don't want or isn't beneficial to us is to unlock our inner self and let it rule both parts. We are like a ship with two different captains and the owner of the ship. A senior captain (the mind), the junior captain (the body) and the owner of the ship (our inner self), a ship with two captains is said to sink but not if they work together. Our mind and body works together most times as I said earlier but even when working together the captains of the ship can sail away to somewhere the owner doesn't want and the owner has to command both captains to take the ship back to where he wants it and they have no choice but to obey, that happens rarely though when your inner self takes charge for a moment and we surprise ourselves and we usually love those moments because we do the right thing well maybe a wrong thing but something we do and have no regrets about, but most times our inner self only whispers to us and we have that strange feeling about a particular thing, some people disregard this feeling some embraces it and wants to always find that feeling before doing anything but usually end up doing what the mind or body wants due to our inner self being suppressed well that's because we haven't united those three parts of us to work as one, when your inner self is awakened your mind and body becomes a loyal follower.

Disciplining the mind and body can only be done by our inner self but it doesn't mean it's awakened, it's more like a situation whereby the ship is in need of something and both captains calls the owner to help fix the situation, both captains having a common goal. Like when we determine to work hard for a better life towards our dreams that decision is made because both the body and mind are going to benefit from it but it isn't always easy because sometimes they'll disagree and fall apart, your body wants the good things of life your mind wants to be at peace and stop having to worry so they both agree to work together to achieve that goal, while at it you get tired and just fall asleep when you shouldn't be sleeping thats the body taking charge and sometimes you just can't stay focus that is your mind taking charge that's probably when your inner self interferes concerning that aspect, being the boss they have no option but to obey, that is when you find yourself fully focused and working tirelessly another example is a smoker who wants to stop smoking, smoking helps the mind relax but the body knows its bad for it but the mind wants it anyway so it automatically overrides the body's choice only way to stop it is to consult our inner self and it gives the order thats when we are able to stay away from it, we usually choke it up to determination.

Ever wondered how the mind that brings up all the crazy stuff we don't want stops just after we tell it we don't want it? The moment you are determined to stop something is when your inner self awakens as I said earlier the few times we are easily able to access our inner self is when we contradict ourself, times like that are when we need our inner self and it intervene because it is needed, that is when you hear two voices in your head most times it goes like "stop I don't want to think that" that's your inner self telling your mind what you don't want. Being able to consult our inner self any time we want can be a bit difficult if we are not attentive to what goes on in our heads. It doesn't need meditation or any kind of hard focusing or anything, as easy as it is to think it can also be that easy to relate with your inner self.

Being able to consult our inner self can help us in all areas of our lives I gave examples on relationships, addictions, even spiritual growth for those who want it being able to relate with our inner self can help a lot in that aspect.

Chapter 2 & 3- Understanding and Connecting to our inner self

Connecting to who we are doesn't need a process or hard focusing of any kind, like I said in the first chapter it just needs attentiveness, when you pay attention to yourself and what goes on in your head and mostly when we are in a tough situation.

Connecting through paying attention can be confusing because you still have to be able to identify which voice is that of our inner self and of the mind, depending on the type of person we've grown into the mind can either be super active or just active which you have to be able to distinguish between the mind and your inner self by the way your mind creates thoughts of its own. Is your mind quick to jump to conclusions and create series of scenarios on a single event ? Or does your mind stays calm till you know for sure what happened relating to a particular event?

I'd like to explain more about it so we know what type of mind we own, how we can identify it and not mistake it for our inner self because they do not have different voice or sound differently, patterns of how they communicate is the only way we can differentiate them.

The super active mind : People with super active minds are mostly impatient people and extremely curious about everything they are interested in, there is a difference in being interested in something and being curious, they are smart people, creative and can also be cunning and have insights on things they've never heard about because of their ability to think fast and create series of expectations. If you posses a mind like this you'll sometimes find yourself explaining something you are hearing for the first time to someone who has known about it for a while.

People with minds like this usually have a busy mind even while talking their mind is coming up with different things at the same time oh I forgot to mention that they forget easily too and the things they remember they remember forever the brain is known to hold memories but the mind is what helps stores and also delete it, so as i was saying people who possess such minds usually have a busy mind it just keeps working like a clock even when they don't want it to, with this kind of mind, if you are very attentive to what goes on in there you'll be able to differentiate your mind from your inner self easily because our inner self is a slow and steady talker it just surfaces gives opinion and go back to its suppression an example is when you are about to do something but having second thoughts about it so you ask yourself if you should do this and your inner self surface and says yes or no depending on whatever it is but it's just speaks once not repetitively like the super active mind so if you pay attention to yourself at that moment you'll hear the voice in your head its more subtle and straightforward, a voice we understand easily not as complex as the mind, gentle and sharp it doesn't sound confused. With this kind of mind it's very easy to distinguish between the mind and your inner self.

The active mind : People with this kind of mind are usually calm and relaxed within because the mind doesn't overthink or brings up something too fast, their mind takes time to assimilate and they process everything that goes in gently with no rush making them understand even more and most times they don't think before talking. I call this kind of mind active because it works well not too slow and not to fast just normal enough to get everything done in due time, people with this mind are brilliant at what they do because their mind is on a stable direction holds things steady and understands everything in that direction unlike the super active mind which brings up ideas and not take enough time to break down the first idea properly before bringing up another one. The active mind is gentle, calm and relaxed and doesn't over work itself which makes it difficult to differentiate from our inner self due to their likeness, the good thing about having this kind of mind is that it makes the best decisions for oneself mostly, the easiest way to distinguish between this kind of mind and our inner self is to understand how your mind brings up things and communicate which is not as easy as it sounds, but possible because our mind works with a pattern which is why it is easy to predict someone's actions sometimes knowing how their mind works. So best shot at differentiating the mind and the inner self is to understand the pattern in which your mind communicates for instance your mind brings up terrible ideas before the goods one pop in or the good ones comes first before the bad ones depends on what type of person you've become through the years either you are optimistic or pessimistic, so if you are an optimistic person with an active mind the good thoughts comes in and the bad ones peep through (no matter how positive we are there usually is that little opening for negativity, shutting it out is what makes us stay more positive) attentiveness will help you figure out which voice is that of your mind and of your inner self.

The simple mind : I didn't mention this kind of mind earlier but I thought it'd be best to discuss every type to help everyone understand what type of mind they own and how they can tell the difference between their mind and their inner self. People with this kind of mind usually find it hard to think outside the box because of its plainness, hardly will you see someone with this kind of mind who isn't 100% trusting, naive, faithful and dangerous, yes dangerous because they lack the ability to think thoroughly so you don't want to piss one off real bad he/she won't think about the consequences or after effects of whatever is going to happen after being through with you 'haha'. The Beauty of this mind is that it comes with lots of surprises, they are not "fools" as many would categorise them as they are just simply made, the simplicity of this kind of mind is what makes it different from the inner self, the voice thats speaks things that scares you is that of your inner self because of the simplicity of your mind complicated things are usually avoided, only your inner self will make you do things that are complicated when you have this kind of mind.

After understanding what type of mind you have, how do you connect with your inner self?

Its simple all you have to do is create a common goal which will suite all three part of you; the body, the mind and your inner self but that isn't possible unless you fully understand who you are i.e your inner self, understanding your inner self will help you know what kind of goal to set that will be of interest to all part of you.

This is where the answer to the question comes in who are you? Like I said in the first chapter who we are may not turn out like we expect depending on the kind of person we've become through the years. For example someone you meet for the first time who seem rather uptight and on getting to know the person better you discover he/she to be a free spirit, but that's not the case here since we are talking about ourselves, discovering who we really are. Over the years we've lived, we have met people who has shaped us to be something either good or bad, experiences that has made us to grow soft or cold the whole journey affects only the body and the mind but never the inner self because it's who we are right from birth.

Understanding who we really are can be a complicated process it requires patience, understanding and full insights into everything that we do and how we react to things that goes on around us.

I was 17 when i first noticed my inner self, i didn't have a lot of friends then so most of my free time was spent exploring my mind, having deep conversations with myself, I wasn't searching for my inner self or anything at that time heck I didn't even knew it existed, it was something I stumbled upon, I noticed the other voice (my inner self) by replaying moments of the day before going to sleep, I would ask myself the first impression i got after seeing something during the day.

The very first time I noticed it was a complete different voice talking in my head was the day an old man came to me begging for money I didn't have so I just looked down and walked away but at that moment in my mind i said i wish i had and would have given it to him so later that day at night i was replaying everything that had happened during the day and when I remembered the old man then what came to my mind about the man occurred to me and it shocked me big time, the exact words were (E ko oshi danu kuro ni waju mi) meaning (get the fuck out of my face), it was completely different from what I thought when i was faced with the man. I kept asking myself how i could say such hateful word i mean i thought i was a nice person but after then I couldn't figure out who I really was anymore because I knew those words didn't just appear from nowhere it must have come from somewhere. Weeks went by I still couldn't figure out where the words came from, it seemed like a stranger inside of me, I decided to pay more attentiveness to everything that went on in my head weeks went by, months went by still nothing but i knew it was somewhere in there then there was this time i was working at a milk factory, being a food processing company they had some pretty strict rules about keeping beards, finger nails and all that i was growing this tiny beard then I didn't like it but I didn't want to remove it also because it made me look a little matured i had a baby face and was working with people atleast 5 years older than i was. There was this day the at work the supervisor noticed my little beard and asked me to get rid of it he was pretty gentle with me because i was obedient and all I think, but his words were "if you don't shave your beards before coming to work tomorrow I'll stop you from working here" right there at that moment i stood up from where i was sitting pulled off my hairnet, gloves, nose mask and uniform and told him I quit and i left, i got home and shaved my tiny beard then I started wondering why i did left if i was still going to shave it because i needed money so bad at that time, like i wasn't thinking when I did that. Most people would paint such actions as teenage rebellion or just a stupid act and rudeness or arrogance but anyone who knew me then would know it had nothing to do with that because i was this gentle kid then.

I knew in my head it was that strange part i was yet to figure out and this time it did a real damage I thought to myself, i was angry at myself for not being able to control what i did, but after a while i was called back to the factory and was apologised to it probably sounds way off for them to apologize since it was a main rule not to keep beards but i was still apologised to because the man said he shouldn't have threatened me and it made me respect that strange part more i felt in its irrational behaviour or thinking it made me earn more respect that I never thought I needed, in essence my innerself reacted roughly because of the threat he made and as time went by I found out it does not take any form of threat lightly.

After then i began to notice the things I do unconsciously not literally unconscious just more of an unexpected action, I understood what makes my innerself pops up, it doesn't always come up when I'm out of options or confused it comes up when I'm in need of it but then i have no idea when exactly because sometimes you feel you have everything all figured out only to find you don't and in moments like that your innerself whispers to you or just takes control.

I got to understand my innerself is an opposite side of who I've made myself to be and it got messy when i was trying to merge both parts because i needed the part of the innerself which was always right about things but i did not know how to cope with the irrational attitude and lack of patience. Trying to merge both parts gave me this double personality when i was 19, i had this friend then who was always caught by surprise everytime I switched up, one moment I'm this nice guy that talks to everyone calmly and the next I'm all rude and stupid "haha" but everytime I switched up it didn't have anything to do with my mood, but as i grew older I came to realize I didn't really need the irrational side of me and how to block it off became tough on me because i was connected to my innerself so i had to settle for one side, i was able to connect to my innerself by understanding the difference between what i do normally and what I wouldn't do in a particular situation, I became more aware of the things I handled differently, the awareness created a bridge connecting me to my innerself. Connecting to our innerself can also be done by creating a common goal that suites all part of us, that way when the body or mind gets tired or feel lazy or not motivated enough to push through, the innerself kicks in creating a regular communication every time it comes up to help, which makes you more familiar to how it motivates you to push through and there you have yourself a steady connection to your innerself which grows as time passes.

Chapter 4 - Accepting who we are

Everything we experience while growing up has shaped who we see ourselves to be now either good or bad, but through everything all our innerself remains intact staying in it's true form making us uniquely different, sometimes experiences makes us want to better ourselves and sometimes it makes us not care about it all living life recklessly, if how we are living at the moment aligns with who we are, it creates a peaceful state of mind, your innerself graciously compliments you everytime and you feel you are finally at peace with yourself, that only happens when you have accepted who you are and not trying to change it but if we are living contrary to who we are then there is this turmoil in us, our innerself keeps criticising what we do not because we are doing the wrong thing, maybe it just doesn't tally with who we are. We are uniquely different but not perfect, as right as our innerself may always be in helping us make decisions even if its a bad one but it gives us satisfaction, it is nowhere near perfect just different, we have to be able to accept who we are knowing pretty well we are far from perfection.

We live in a world where people expect you to be good always and do things right always but I believe there is no one way to do things you are either doing it or not, if it was possible for everyone to be good there wouldn't be people in skins of different colours but just one colour, it is okay to be good it is also okay to be bad you just have to accept who you are and be happy with who you are, it's your life the choice of bettering yourself is yours, choosing to affect the people around you positively or negatively is yours and in your capability alone, you want to be a good person it's totally okay you want to be bad it is totally okay you can be bad and also affect the people around you positively you can be good and affect people around you negatively, letting society decide how your life is lived is totally wrong, accepting that you are far from perfection is how you can find peace internally and that alone can make you affect people around you positively, you don't have to be good to be able to do good things, bad people do good things, good people do bad things.

Be good and proud, be bad and proud don't pretend to be bad when you are good and don't pretend to be good when you are bad. Being good or bad isn't a summary of who we are,infact there is no one word to define who we are. we can neither be good nor bad, we are who we are, we all posses good and bad characteristics, i am only using the word good and bad to create a better understanding being there are billions of people on earth who are uniquely different.

Chapter 5 - Building our innerself

As humans, imperfections are our perfection. How we live each day of our lives contributes to our experiences, striving to be better than we were yesterday. Becoming aware of who we are creates an opportunity for us to be able to better ourselves.

As I've written in the previous chapter who we are doesn't always turn out as we expect, sometimes discovering who we really are can leave us disturbed and troubled, in situations like that we tend to think of how to better ourselves or run from it but the better option is to face it and build ourself to how we want it, our innerself isn't a part of us that can be shaped into what we want whenever we want or however we want, its the part of us that holds our true personality not one shaped from experiences but from birth which is why to better ourselves we need a part of us that was also birthed with us, which is our mind. The mind has the ability to help build us properly if accessed the right way through meditation.

There are different types of meditation, i am not particularly familiarised with any but there is this particular type that helps in building the inner self not only the innerself infact it helps awaken the positive qualities buried within us, i came across the full details of the meditation type on some website.

This type of meditation is called Raja yoga meditation, I'm going to take bits of the article that explains the advantages of the meditation and insert in this chapter but for better understanding I'll suggest to visit the website to read in full.

The Raja yoga meditation: *"Raja Yoga meditation is a technique mentioned in the Bhagavad Gita, popularized by Swami Vivekananda in the 19th century.*

Since then, it has gained popularity and is widely taught around the world to maintain mind stability and sanity. The meditation is named 'raja' because the practice aims to impart king-like qualities of confidence, awareness, and independence.

This technique is a spiritual process to know yourself better, and it uses the power of the mind to control the body. It awakens the positive qualities buried within you, enabling better performance, and teaches the importance of silence and introspection. Raja Yoga meditation is spiritual and preaches that all religions have a common ground – spirituality.

- *Raja Yoga meditation gives peace of mind and relaxes the body*

- *It helps develop a positive attitude and respond better to situations*

- *This meditation helps develop positive relationships*

- *It improves concentration and increases clarity*

- *A broad sense of self-worth is developed*

- *It helps find purpose in life and work towards it*

- *You feel content and stable*

• You will experience peace, and there will be an improvement in health."
— stylecraze.com

The Raja yoga meditation : *"Raja Yoga meditation is a form of meditation that is accessible to people of all backgrounds. It is a meditation without rituals or mantras and can be practised anywhere at any time. Raja Yoga meditation is practised with 'open eyes', which makes this method of meditation versatile, simple and easy to practice. Meditation is a state of being in that place just beyond every day consciousness, which is where spiritual empowerment begins. Spiritual*

awareness gives us the power to choose good and positive thoughts over those which are negative and wasteful. We start to respond to situations, rather than just reacting to them. We begin to live with harmony, we create better and happier, healthier relationships and change our lives in a most positive way."
— brahmakumaris.org

The Raja yoga meditation: " *Raja Yoga means yoga to become a king – a master over yourself. It also means union with God. The aim of Raja Yoga is to discipline the mind, sharpen the intellect and to have full control over the bodily senses. It is an ancient open-eyed meditation technique which comes from India and is free to learn. It is a great way to save your time, energy and money as it makes you wiser and more in control of your life as you develop will power. One truly can become a self-ruler.“* — inspiredstillness.com

The Raja yoga meditation: “ *Raja yoga, is the royal path of meditation. As a king maintains control over his kingdom, so can we maintain control over our own “kingdom”. “* — vedanta.org

Following the step by step guides on these websites we can learn to meditate on our own or we can contact a teacher to help guide us but however we choose to learn the results will first be visible to us alone before reflecting to the people around us.